SPACE SCIENCE

VENUS

BY BETSY RATHBURN

BELLWETHER MEDIA ∘ MINNEAPOLIS, MN

TM

Are you ready to take it to the extreme? Torque books thrust you into the action-packed world of sports, vehicles, mystery, and adventure. These books may include dirt, smoke, fire, and chilling tales. **WARNING**: read at your own risk.

This edition first published in 2019 by Bellwether Media, Inc.

Library of Congress Cataloging-in-Publication Data

Names: Rathburn, Betsy, author.
Title: Venus / by Betsy Rathburn.
Description: Minneapolis, MN : Bellwether Media, Inc., [2019] |
    Series: Torque. Space Science | Audience: Ages 7-12. |
    Audience: Grades 3 to 7. | Includes bibliographical references and index.
Identifiers: LCCN 2018039170 (print) | LCCN 2018040548 (ebook) | ISBN
    9781681036984 (ebook) | ISBN 9781626179806 (hardcover : alk. paper)
Subjects: LCSH: Venus (Planet)–Juvenile literature.
Classification: LCC QB621 (ebook) | LCC QB621 .R375 2019 (print) |
    DDC 523.42–dc23
LC record available at https://lccn.loc.gov/2018039170

Editor: Kate Moening   Designer: Andrea Schneider

Printed in the United States of America, North Mankato, MN.

TABLE OF CONTENTS

THE BRIGHTEST LIGHT

It is a chilly fall evening just after sunset. A **new moon** makes the sky dark. The only light comes from the stars twinkling above.

As the sky blackens, a bright dot of light becomes visible. It is the brightest object in the moonless sky. This is Venus!

VENUS

HELP FROM THE SUN

Venus looks bright in the night sky because of sunlight bouncing off its clouds!

WHAT IS VENUS?

Venus is the solar system's third-smallest planet. Only Mars and Mercury are smaller. At 7,500 miles (12,070 kilometers) across, Venus is a little smaller than Earth.

This planet is named after the Roman goddess of love and beauty. It usually appears just before sunrise or just after sunset. This is why it is sometimes called the Morning Star or Evening Star.

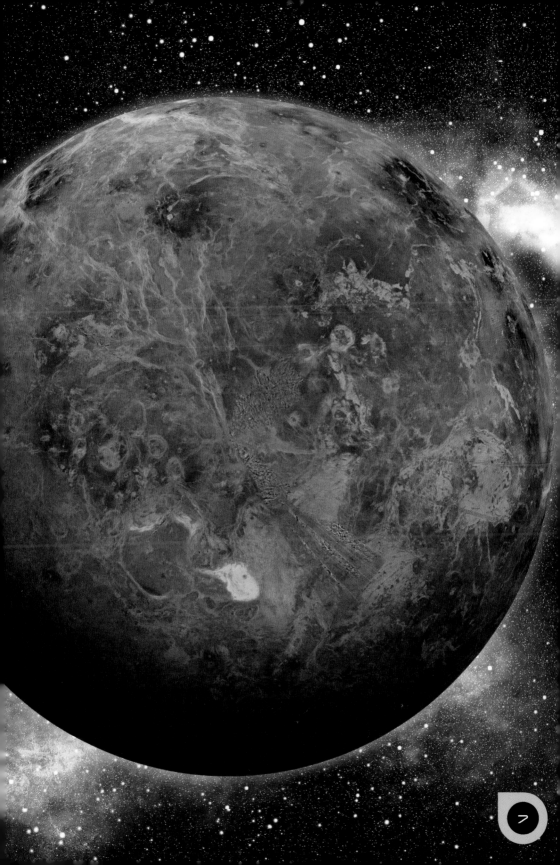

FUN FACT

TOXIC AIR

Venus's atmosphere is made mostly of sulfuric acid and carbon dioxide gas. These materials are deadly to humans and most animals!

Venus is the hottest planet in the solar system! Its surface reaches more than 800 degrees Fahrenheit (482 degrees Celsius).

The heat is caused by the planet's thick **atmosphere**. It is made up of gases that trap heat from the Sun. This is called the **greenhouse effect**.

VENUS PASSING IN
FRONT OF THE SUN

FUN FACT

UP IN THE AIR

The surface of Venus is much too hot for life.
But some scientists think there could be life
in the planet's clouds!

From afar, Venus looks like it is covered in
brown and white swirls. These are clouds in
the planet's atmosphere. They hide a rocky
surface covered in mountains and **volcanoes**.

MAAT MONS

Many of the planet's volcanoes are very tall. The largest is Maat Mons. It rises 5 miles (8 kilometers) high! But scientists believe many of Venus's volcanoes are no longer active.

HOW DID VENUS FORM?

About 4.6 billion years ago, the solar system was a cloud of dust and gas. In time, **gravity** caused the materials to cave in. The Sun formed in the center.

Rocky planets like Venus grew from leftover pieces of dust and rock. Gravity pulled the materials into a **core**. As time passed, a **crust** formed around the core.

ILLUSTRATION OF A
PLANET FORMING

FUN FACT

ANCIENT OCEANS

Scientists believe Venus was once covered by a giant ocean. The planet also had much cooler temperatures. This means the surface may have been able to support life!

Venus's surface looks much different today than when it first formed. Over millions of years, mountains and volcanoes pushed through the planet's crust. Deep valleys formed between them.

MEAD, VENUS'S
LARGEST CRATER

Venus has fewer **craters** than other rocky planets. The craters it does have are huge! This is because **meteorites** must be very big to survive Venus's atmosphere. Venus's largest crater is about 170 miles (274 kilometers) across!

WHERE IS VENUS FOUND?

Venus is the second-closest planet to the Sun. It **orbits** the star from about 67 million miles (108 million kilometers) away. The journey takes 225 days.

As Venus orbits the Sun, it spins. Most planets spin **counter-clockwise**. But Venus spins in the opposite direction. It takes 243 days to complete one **rotation**. That means that on Venus, a day is longer than a year!

HOW FAR AWAY IS VENUS?

EARTH TO VENUS = 26,000,000 MILES
(41,800,000 KILOMETERS)

VENUS TO SUN = 67,000,000 MILES
(108,000,000 KILOMETERS)

WHY DO WE STUDY VENUS?

Venus is known as Earth's twin. These close neighbors are about the same size. Scientists study Venus to learn more about Earth. They compare how the two planets formed.

Studying Venus can tell us what Earth's future might hold. If Earth's atmosphere traps too much heat, our planet may one day look like Venus!

EARTH VS. VENUS

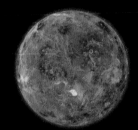

SIZE: 7,918 miles
(12,743 kilometers) across

ATMOSPHERE: mostly
oxygen and nitrogen gases

AVERAGE TEMPERATURE:
58.3 degrees Fahrenheit
(14.6 degrees Celsius)

LENGTH OF DAY:
about 24 hours

LENGTH OF YEAR:
about 365 days

SIZE: 7,500 miles
(12,070 kilometers) across

ATMOSPHERE: mostly
carbon dioxide gas

AVERAGE TEMPERATURE:
900 degrees Fahrenheit
(482 degrees Celsius)

LENGTH OF DAY:
5,382 hours, or 243 days

LENGTH OF YEAR:
225 Earth days

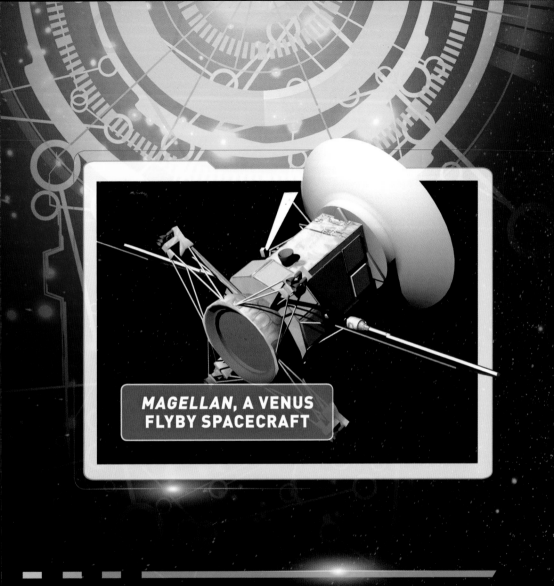

MAGELLAN, A VENUS
FLYBY SPACECRAFT

It is hard to study Venus. Its atmosphere
and temperature make it hard for **probes**
to survive. Past Venus probes lasted less
than an hour!

More research will help scientists build better Venus probes. **Flyby** spacecraft may study the gases that make up the planet's atmosphere. In the future, we may know as much about Earth's twin as we do about Earth!

GLOSSARY

atmosphere—the gases that surround Venus and other planets

core—the innermost part of Venus

counter-clockwise—in the opposite direction that the hands of a clock turn

craters—deep holes in the surface of an object

crust—the uppermost part of Venus's surface

flyby—a spacecraft flight that does not land but is close enough to collect scientific information

gravity—the force that pulls objects toward one another

greenhouse effect—the warming of the atmosphere caused by energy from the Sun

meteorites—pieces of asteroids that make it through a planet's atmosphere

new moon—the phase of the moon when its dark side faces Earth

orbits—moves around something in a fixed path

probes—spacecraft designed to study faraway objects in space

rotation—Venus's turning on its axis

volcanoes—vents that let out hot rocks and steam

TO LEARN MORE

AT THE LIBRARY

Berne, Emma Carlson. *The Secrets of Venus*. North Mankato, Minn.: Capstone Press, 2016.

Goldstein, Margaret J. *Discover Venus*. Minneapolis, Minn.: Lerner Publications, 2019.

Payment, Simone. *Venus*. New York, N.Y.: Britannica Educational Publishing, 2017.

ON THE WEB

FACTSURFER

Factsurfer.com gives you a safe, fun way to find more information.

1. Go to www.factsurfer.com.

2. Enter "Venus" into the search box.

3. Click the "Surf" button and select your book cover to see a list of related web sites.

INDEX

The images in this book are reproduced through the courtesy of: NASA images, front cover, p. 2; Kim Christensen / Alamy Stock Photo/ Alamy, pp. 4-5; NASA/JPL/ NASA Images, pp. 6-7; NASA Images/ NASA Images, pp. 8-9; NASA - Jet Propulsion Laboratory/ Wikipedia, pp. 10-11; Mopic, pp. 12-13; Ron Miller / Stocktrek Images/ Alamy, pp. 14-15; NASA/JPL/ NASA Images, p. 15 (inset); Vitaly Sosnovskiy, p. 17 (Sun); Vadim Sadovski, pp. 17, 18-19 (Venus); Elenarts, pp. 18-19 (Earth), 20 (inset); janez volmajer, p. 21.